10 Interesting Facts About Marrakech

A Collection of Amazing Facts About Marrakech

Introduction

Welcome to Marrakech, a city steeped in history, vibrant colors, and the energy of its bustling souks and ancient palaces. In "100 Amazing Facts About Marrakech for Young Readers," you're about to embark on a journey through narrow alleys filled with the scent of spices, past ornate gates that lead to hidden gardens, and into a city where tradition meets modernity.

Join us as we uncover Marrakech's rich cultural tapestry, its flavorsome cuisine, and the warmth of its people. Whether you're intrigued by the intricate craftsmanship of its artisans or curious about the city's vibrant festivals, this book promises to ignite your curiosity and transport you to a world where history, culture, and adventure await at every turn. Let's dive into the magic of Marrakech together!

Chapter 1: Introduction to Marrakech

Fact 1: Geographic Location

Fact 2: Key Landmarks

Fact 3: Surrounding Regions

Fact 4: Proximity to Atlas Mountains

Fact 5: Accessibility

Fact 1: Geographic Location

Marrakech is located in the western part of Morocco, nestled at the foothills of the majestic Atlas Mountains. The city is strategically situated about 327 kilometers (203 miles) southwest of the capital, Rabat, making it a central hub for travelers exploring the country. Its prime location allows easy access to both mountain adventures and desert excursions.

Fact 2: Key Landmarks

Marrakech is known for its prominent red sandstone walls and buildings, which have earned it the nickname "The Red City." The Medina is a vibrant maze of narrow alleyways filled with history and culture. Its bustling souks offer a sensory overload of sights, sounds, and scents, from colorful spices to traditional crafts. Walking through the Medina, visitors can discover centuries-old palaces, mosques, and hidden courtyards that reflect Marrakech's rich heritage.

Fact 3: Surrounding Regions

The city is surrounded by diverse landscapes, including fertile plains and arid desert regions. This unique setting provides a variety of experiences for visitors, from exploring lush gardens to embarking on desert adventures. Nearby, the picturesque Ourika Valley offers scenic hikes and traditional Berber villages. Additionally, the Agafay Desert, with its rocky terrain and expansive vistas, provides an unforgettable backdrop for camel rides and stargazing.

Fact 4: Proximity to Atlas Mountains

Marrakech's close proximity to the Atlas Mountains makes it an ideal starting point for trekking and outdoor activities. The mountains provide a stunning backdrop to the city's bustling streets and offer a cool escape from the urban heat. Adventurers can explore scenic trails, waterfalls, and traditional Berber villages nestled in the mountains. During winter, the Oukaimeden Ski Resort in the High Atlas offers a unique skiing experience close to Marrakech.

Fact 5: Accessibility

Marrakech is well-connected by road, rail, and air. The Marrakech-Menara Airport serves as a major gateway for international tourists, while extensive road networks link the city to other major Moroccan destinations. The efficient train system connects Marrakech to cities like Casablanca and Tangier, offering convenient travel options for both locals and visitors exploring Morocco.

Chapter 2: Historical Highlights

Fact 6: Founding of Marrakech

Fact 7: Historical Monuments

Fact 8: Influences of Different Dynasties

Fact 9: Key Historical Events

Fact 10: Modern History

Fact 6: Founding of Marrakech

Marrakech was founded in 1062 by Abu Bakr ibn Umar, a chieftain and cousin of the Almoravid ruler. Its strategic location near the Atlas Mountains and major trade routes contributed to its rapid growth as a cultural center. This establishment marked the beginning of Marrakech's significant role in history, influencing trade and culture throughout the medieval period.

Fact 7: Historical Monuments

Marrakech boasts a wealth of historical monuments, including the Koutoubia Mosque, built in the 12th century, renowned for its iconic minaret and stunning architecture that reflects the Almohad dynasty's influence. This mosque not only serves as a prominent religious center but also stands as a symbol of Marrakech's architectural prowess and cultural heritage, drawing admiration from visitors and historians alike for its intricate craftsmanship and historical significance.

Fact 8. Influences of Different Dynasties

The city's history is shaped by various dynasties, such as the Almoravids, Almohads, and Saadians, each leaving their mark through architectural marvels, urban planning, and cultural practices that define Marrakech's unique identity. Their contributions are evident in the intricate tilework of mosques, the layout of bustling souks, and the preservation of traditional arts and crafts that continue to thrive in the city today.

Fact 9: Key Historical Events

Key historical events in Marrakech's timeline include the establishment of the Saadian dynasty in the 16th century, which marked a period of cultural and economic prosperity, and the French Protectorate era in the early 20th century, influencing modern development. These events shaped Marrakech's cultural evolution, leaving lasting legacies visible in its architecture, governance, and societal norms.

Fact 10: Modern History

In modern times, Marrakech has emerged as a global tourist destination, blending its rich historical heritage with modern amenities and international influences, attracting visitors from around the world to experience its vibrant culture and traditions. Its bustling markets, luxurious riads, and diverse culinary scene contribute to its allure as a must-visit destination for travelers seeking both authenticity and luxury in their experiences.

Chapter 3: Natural Wonders

- Fact 11. Atlas Mountains

- Fact 12. Ourika Valley

- Fact 13. Agafay Desert

- Fact 14. Menara Gardens

- Fact 15. Majorelle Garden

Fact 11: Atlas Mountains

The Atlas Mountains are a stunning range near Marrakech, known for their breathtaking landscapes and high peaks. Mount Toubkal, the highest peak at 4,167 meters (13,671 feet), is a popular destination for hikers and climbers. The mountains are also home to vibrant Berber villages. Visitors to Marrakech can easily arrange trips to explore these majestic mountains and their natural beauty.

Fact 12. Ourika Valley

Located in the High Atlas Mountains, the Ourika Valley is known for its lush greenery, terraced gardens, and traditional Berber villages. It's a popular destination for day trips from Marrakech, offering scenic hikes to waterfalls and insights into Berber culture. Visitors can explore picturesque landscapes, visit local craft workshops, and enjoy traditional mint tea with Berber families, creating memorable experiences amidst stunning natural beauty.

Fact 13. Agafay Desert

The Agafay Desert, near Marrakech, is a rocky desert landscape offering a serene escape from the city. Visitors can experience camel rides, stargazing under clear desert skies, and cultural experiences with local Berber communities. This tranquil desert environment provides a peaceful retreat where travelers can immerse themselves in traditional Berber hospitality, enjoy traditional music around campfires, and witness mesmerizing sunsets over the arid landscape.

Fact 14. Menara Gardens

The Menara Gardens, established in the 12th century by the Almohad dynasty, feature a tranquil olive grove surrounding a large reflecting pool. It's a favorite spot for locals and visitors to relax amidst stunning views of the Atlas Mountains. This historic site offers a serene atmosphere where visitors can stroll along shaded pathways, admire the ancient olive trees, and enjoy picnics by the reflective pool, all while soaking in the beauty of Marrakech's natural surroundings.

Fact 15. Majorelle Garden

Created by French painter Jacques Majorelle, the Majorelle Garden is a botanical oasis in Marrakech. It features exotic plants, vibrant blue buildings, and a Berber Museum showcasing North African textiles and artifacts, offering a peaceful retreat from the city's bustling streets. This tranquil haven also includes fountains, streams, and pathways adorned with colorful pottery, creating a harmonious blend of art, nature, and cultural heritage that captivates visitors from around the world.

Chapter 4: Cultural Heritage

- Fact 16: Traditional Moroccan Art

- Fact 17: Music and Dance

- Fact 18: Handicrafts and Souks

- Fact 19: Festivals and Celebrations

- Fact 20: Culinary Traditions

Fact 16: Traditional Moroccan Art

Moroccan art is renowned for its intricate geometric patterns, vibrant colors, and skilled craftsmanship seen in pottery, textiles, and woodwork. Influenced by Berber, Arab, and Andalusian traditions, it reflects Morocco's rich cultural diversity and historical influences. This artistic heritage is preserved through meticulous techniques passed down through generations, blending traditional motifs with contemporary interpretations that continue to captivate admirers worldwide.

Fact 17: Music and Dance

Moroccan music and dance encompass a variety of styles, from the rhythmic beats of Gnawa music to the lively rhythms of chaabi. Traditional instruments like the oud and bendir accompany ceremonial celebrations and social gatherings, embodying the country's cultural expressions. These musical traditions are deeply rooted in Morocco's history, evolving over centuries to reflect regional diversity and societal changes, yet retaining their essential role in communal festivities and artistic storytelling.

Fact 18. Handicrafts and Souks

Morocco's souks are vibrant marketplaces where artisans sell handmade goods such as leather goods, carpets, and metalwork. Each city specializes in unique crafts, such as the intricate embroidery of Fes or the pottery of Safi, preserving centuries-old techniques and traditions. These bustling markets are not just places of commerce but also cultural hubs where stories, skills, and heritage are exchanged and celebrated daily.

Fact 19. Festivals and Celebrations

Morocco celebrates a rich tapestry of festivals, from religious events like Eid al-Fitr to cultural celebrations like the Festival of Roses in Kelaa M'Gouna. These festivals showcase music, dance, and culinary delights, inviting locals and visitors alike to experience Morocco's festive spirit. They serve as vibrant showcases of Moroccan identity and cultural heritage, fostering community spirit and unity across diverse regions and traditions.

Fact 20. Culinary Traditions

Moroccan cuisine is a blend of flavors from Berber, Arab, and Mediterranean influences, featuring dishes like tagine, couscous, and pastilla. Ingredients like spices, olives, and preserved lemons add depth to traditional meals enjoyed in homes, street stalls, and elegant restaurants across the country. This culinary diversity reflects Morocco's history as a crossroads of cultures, where food is not just sustenance but a cherished part of social gatherings and cultural identity.

Chapter 5: Places to Visit in Marrakech

- Fact 21: Jemaa el-Fnaa

- Fact 22: Koutoubia Mosque

- Fact 23: Bahia Palace

- Fact 24: Saadian Tombs

- Fact 25: El Badi Palace

Fact 21: Jemaa el-Fnaa

Jemaa el-Fnaa is Marrakech's main square, renowned for its vibrant atmosphere. During the day, it's bustling with food stalls offering Moroccan delicacies, storytellers recounting tales of old, and snake charmers captivating passersby. As dusk falls, the square transforms into a lively entertainment hub with musicians playing traditional instruments like the oud and guembri, and dancers performing to rhythmic beats, creating an unforgettable spectacle under the stars.

Fact 22. Koutoubia Mosque

Built in the 12th century, the Koutoubia Mosque stands as Marrakech's largest mosque, celebrated for its iconic minaret that towers above the cityscape. An architectural masterpiece of the Almohad dynasty, it showcases exquisite geometric patterns and intricate details in its design. The mosque not only serves as a spiritual center for worship but also as a cultural landmark that symbolizes Marrakech's rich history and enduring architectural legacy.

Fact 23: Bahia Palace

Bahia Palace, meaning "Brilliance," is a 19th-century palace that exemplifies Islamic and Moroccan architectural styles. Its intricately decorated rooms, lush gardens, and serene courtyards offer a glimpse into the opulent lifestyle of Moroccan royalty. The palace features stunning mosaics, carved woodwork, and stucco decorations, reflecting the exquisite craftsmanship of the era. Visiting Bahia Palace allows one to experience the grandeur and elegance that characterized the lives of Morocco's elite during the 19th century.

Fact 24: Saadian Tombs

The Saadian Tombs are mausoleums dating back to the Saadian dynasty, rediscovered in the early 20th century. They are renowned for their stunning Hispano-Moorish architecture and intricate tile work, housing the tombs of Saadian rulers and their families. Nestled within a lush garden, the tombs are a testament to the dynasty's architectural and artistic achievements, attracting historians and tourists alike who seek to explore Marrakech's regal past.

Fact 25: El Badi Palace

El Badi Palace, meaning "The Incomparable," was built in the late 16th century by Sultan Ahmad al-Mansur. Though now mostly in ruins, its vast courtyard and towering walls evoke the grandeur of its original construction, offering panoramic views of the city. Once a lavish complex adorned with gold, marble, and precious materials, it remains a symbol of Marrakech's historical opulence and architectural prowess.

Chapter 6: Travel Tips for Marrakech

- Fact 26: Best Time to Visit

- Fact 27: Getting Around Marrakech

- Fact 28: Safety Tips for Tourists

- Fact 29: Local Etiquette

- Fact 30: Sustainable Travel Practices

Fact 26: Best Time to Visit

The best time to visit Marrakech is during the spring (March to May) and autumn (September to November) when the weather is mild and pleasant. These seasons offer comfortable temperatures for exploring the city's outdoor attractions and vibrant markets without the extreme heat of summer or the cool nights of winter. Additionally, these periods coincide with various cultural festivals and events, providing a richer experience of the city's vibrant heritage.

Fact 27: Getting Around Marrakech

Navigating Marrakech is easiest on foot, especially within the Medina's narrow streets. For longer distances, taxis and horse-drawn carriages (calèches) are popular options. It's advisable to agree on a fare before starting your journey to avoid misunderstandings. Buses and the Marrakech City Tour tourist bus provide additional transportation options for exploring the city.

Fact 28: Safety Tips for Tourists

Marrakech is generally safe for tourists, but it's important to stay vigilant, especially in crowded areas like Jemaa el-Fnaa. Keep your belongings secure and be aware of your surroundings. Avoid walking alone late at night and be cautious of scams and overly persistent street vendors. Always use official taxis and avoid unlicensed transport. It's also advisable to have a copy of your passport and important documents in case of emergencies.

Fact 29: Local Etiquette

Respect local customs and traditions when visiting Marrakech. Dress modestly, especially when visiting religious sites, and avoid public displays of affection. It's polite to greet locals with "Salam Alaikum" and use your right hand for eating and giving or receiving items. Haggling is common in markets, so engage in friendly negotiations when shopping. Additionally, always ask for permission before taking photos of people, especially in the Medina and markets.

Fact 30: Sustainable Travel Practices

To travel sustainably in Marrakech, choose eco-friendly accommodations that support local communities. Reduce your environmental impact by using reusable water bottles and shopping bags. Support local artisans by purchasing handmade goods and avoid products made from endangered species. Be mindful of water and energy usage, and participate in responsible tourism activities that promote cultural preservation and environmental conservation.

Chapter 7: Famous Cities and Regions in Morocco

- Fact 31: Casablanca

- Fact 32: Rabat

- Fact 33: Fes

- Fact 34: Tangier

- Fact 35: Chefchaouen

Fact 31: Casablanca

Casablanca, Morocco's largest city, is an economic hub and modern metropolis. Known for its stunning blend of traditional and contemporary architecture, the city is home to the Hassan II Mosque, one of the largest mosques in the world. Its vibrant nightlife, upscale restaurants, and shopping districts make it a dynamic and cosmopolitan destination.

Fact 32: Rabat

Rabat, the capital city of Morocco, is a blend of historical and modern attractions. It features the ancient Kasbah of the Udayas, the grand Royal Palace, and the Hassan Tower, an unfinished minaret from the 12th century. With its coastal location, Rabat offers beautiful beaches, gardens, and a more relaxed atmosphere compared to other major cities. The city also hosts numerous cultural festivals and events, celebrating its rich heritage and vibrant arts scene.

Fact 33 : Fes

Fes is one of Morocco's most culturally and spiritually significant cities, known for its well-preserved medieval architecture. The Fes el-Bali, the old medina, is a UNESCO World Heritage site, filled with narrow alleys, vibrant souks, and the historic University of Al Quaraouiyine, considered the oldest existing educational institution in the world. Fes is a center for traditional crafts, including leatherwork and ceramics.

Fact 34 : Tangier

Tangier, located at the northern tip of Morocco, is a city with a rich history and a unique blend of cultures due to its proximity to Europe. Known for its beautiful beaches, bustling port, and historic medina, Tangier has long been a gateway between Africa and Europe. The city's charming cafes, vibrant markets, and cultural landmarks, such as the Kasbah Museum, reflect its diverse heritage.

Fact 35: Chefchaouen

Chefchaouen, often called the "Blue City," is famous for its stunning blue-painted streets and buildings. Nestled in the Rif Mountains, this picturesque town offers a serene escape with its relaxed atmosphere, charming medina, and scenic views. Chefchaouen is also known for its artisanal products, including woven blankets and handmade crafts, making it a favorite destination for tourists seeking a unique and tranquil experience.

Chapter 8: Architecture in Marrakech

- Fact 36: Education SystemMoorish Architecture

- Fact 37: Riads and Courtyards

- Fact 38: Medina of Marrakech

- Fact 39: Modern Buildings

- Fact 40: Historical Fortifications

Fact 36: Moorish Architecture

Marrakech is renowned for its stunning Moorish architecture, characterized by intricate tilework, horseshoe arches, and ornate plasterwork. This style, influenced by Islamic art and Andalusian aesthetics, is evident in many of the city's historic buildings and monuments. Notable examples include the Koutoubia Mosque and the Ben Youssef Madrasa.

Fact 37: Riads and Courtyards

Riads, traditional Moroccan houses with central courtyards, are a hallmark of Marrakech's architecture. These serene spaces often feature lush gardens, fountains, and intricate tile mosaics, offering a peaceful retreat from the bustling streets. Many riads have been converted into boutique hotels, providing visitors with an authentic Moroccan experience.

Fact 38: Medina of Marrakech

The Medina of Marrakech is a labyrinth of narrow alleyways and traditional buildings. Its architecture reflects centuries of history, with structures dating back to the Almoravid and Saadian dynasties, showcasing a blend of Islamic and Berber influences. The Medina is home to bustling souks, historic mosques, and beautifully restored riads.

Fact 39: Modern Buildings

While Marrakech is steeped in history, it also embraces modern architecture. Contemporary structures like the Menara Mall and luxury hotels blend traditional Moroccan design elements with modern aesthetics, creating a unique architectural landscape. These buildings often incorporate innovative designs while respecting the city's cultural heritage.

Fact 40: Historical Fortifications

Marrakech's historical fortifications include the iconic city walls and gates, such as Bab Agnaou and Bab Doukkala. Built in the 12th century, these structures served as defensive barriers and are adorned with intricate carvings and decorative elements, reflecting the city's rich architectural heritage. The walls stretch for kilometers, enclosing the historic Medina and protecting it from invaders.

Chapter 9: Markets and Souks

- Fact 41: Souk Semmarine

- Fact 42: Spice Market

- Fact 43: Leather Tanneries

- Fact 44: Artisan Workshops

- Fact 45: Local Bazaars

Fact 41: Souk Semmarine

Souk Semmarine is one of the largest and most vibrant markets in Marrakech's Medina. This bustling souk is known for its wide array of goods, including textiles, lanterns, ceramics, and jewelry. It's a popular spot for both locals and tourists, offering a sensory overload of colors, sounds, and smells. Wandering through its maze-like alleys, visitors can find unique handcrafted items and immerse themselves in the lively atmosphere of Marrakech's traditional market culture.

Fact 42: The Viking Ship Museum

The Spice Market, also known as Rahba Kedima, is a must-visit for anyone interested in the flavors and aromas of Moroccan cuisine. Here, you'll find an array of spices piled high in colorful mounds, from saffron and cumin to paprika and turmeric. Vendors often provide samples and explanations of the various spices and their uses.

Fact 43: Leather Tanneries

The leather tanneries of Marrakech, such as the ones in Bab Debbagh, are famous for their traditional methods of leather production. Visitors can observe the fascinating and labor-intensive process of tanning hides, which involves soaking, dyeing, and drying the leather. The vibrant colors of the dye pits create a striking visual contrast against the surrounding buildings.

Fact 44: Artisan Workshops

Marrakech is home to numerous artisan workshops where skilled craftsmen create traditional Moroccan goods. These workshops produce items like intricate metalwork, handwoven textiles, and beautifully painted ceramics. Visiting these workshops provides insight into the time-honored techniques passed down through generations.

Fact 45: Local Bazaars

Local bazaars in Marrakech offer a more intimate shopping experience compared to the larger souks. These smaller markets, scattered throughout the Medina, are perfect for discovering unique, handcrafted items. From handmade slippers to traditional Moroccan lamps, local bazaars provide a treasure trove of authentic souvenirs and gifts.

Chapter 10: Daily Life in Marrakech

- Fact 46: Traditional Clothing

- Fact 47: Transportation in Norway

- Fact 48: Family Life

- Fact 49: Education System

- Fact 50: Sports and Recreation

Fact 46: Traditional Clothing

Traditional clothing in Marrakech reflects the city's rich cultural heritage. Men often wear djellabas, long loose-fitting robes with hoods, while women might wear caftans adorned with intricate embroidery. During special occasions and festivals, people dress in more elaborate traditional attire, showcasing the vibrant patterns and colors that are characteristic of Moroccan fashion.

Fact 47: Local Cuisine

Marrakech's local cuisine is a flavorful blend of spices, fresh ingredients, and time-honored cooking techniques. Popular dishes include tagine, a slow-cooked stew made with meat, vegetables, and aromatic spices, and couscous, a staple grain served with a variety of toppings. Street food, such as grilled meats, fresh bread, and sweet pastries, is also a vital part of the city's culinary landscape.

Fact 48: Family Life

Family life in Marrakech is deeply rooted in tradition and community. Extended families often live close to each other, and family gatherings are frequent and cherished. Respect for elders is a significant aspect of Moroccan culture, and children are raised with strong family values. Meals are often shared, and special occasions like weddings and holidays bring families together in celebration.

Fact 49: Education System

The education system in Marrakech, like in the rest of Morocco, includes primary, secondary, and higher education. Schools often teach in both Arabic and French, and there is a growing emphasis on learning English. In addition to public schools, there are private and international schools that offer a diverse range of educational opportunities. Higher education institutions, such as universities, provide advanced studies in various fields.

Fact 50: Sports and Recreation

Sports and recreation are an important part of daily life in Marrakech. Football (soccer) is the most popular sport, with many locals participating in and watching matches. Other common activities include jogging, cycling, and traditional Moroccan sports like tbourida (equestrian performance). Public parks and gardens, such as the Menara Gardens, offer spaces for leisure and exercise, contributing to the city's vibrant community life.

Chapter 11: Nature and Wildlife

- Fact 51: High Atlas Wildlife

- Fact 52: Birds of Marrakech

- Fact 53: Desert Flora

- Fact 54: Endangered Species

- Fact 55: Conservation Efforts

Fact 51: High Atlas Wildlife

The High Atlas Mountains, located near Marrakech, are home to a diverse range of wildlife. This mountainous region hosts species such as Barbary macaques, Atlas deer, and a variety of reptiles. The unique climate and varied habitats of the High Atlas support rich biodiversity, making it a vital area for wildlife conservation.

Fact 52: Birds of Marrakech

Marrakech is a haven for birdwatchers, with many species inhabiting the city and surrounding areas. Birds such as the white stork, common bulbul, and house sparrow are frequently seen. Additionally, the nearby wetlands and gardens attract migratory birds, providing excellent opportunities for observing a wide variety of avian species.

Fact 53: Desert Flora

The desert regions surrounding Marrakech are characterized by hardy, drought-resistant plants. Species like date palms, cacti, and acacia trees are well-adapted to the arid environment. These plants play a crucial role in preventing soil erosion and supporting the desert ecosystem by providing food and shelter for various wildlife species.

Fact 54: Endangered Species

Morocco is home to several endangered species, and Marrakech's surrounding areas are no exception. The Barbary leopard, Cuvier's gazelle, and the critically endangered Moroccan tortoise are some of the species at risk. Conservation efforts are essential to protect these animals and their habitats from further decline.

Fact 55: Conservation Efforts

Conservation efforts in Marrakech and its surrounding regions focus on protecting biodiversity and promoting sustainable practices. Initiatives include habitat restoration, wildlife protection laws, and environmental education programs. Organizations work alongside local communities to ensure the preservation of natural resources and the survival of endangered species, fostering a balance between human activity and nature conservation.

Chapter 12: Economy and Trade

- Fact 56: Historical Trade Routes

- Fact 57: Modern Industries

- Fact 58: Tourism Economy

- Fact 59: Artisan Crafts

- Fact 60: Local Markets

Fact 56: Historical Trade Routes

Marrakech historically played a crucial role in trade, serving as a key hub on the trans-Saharan trade routes. Caravans transported goods such as gold, salt, and spices from sub-Saharan Africa to the Mediterranean and Europe. This trade brought wealth and diverse cultural influences, shaping Marrakech into a vibrant, cosmopolitan city.

Fact 57: Modern Industries

Today, Marrakech's economy is diversified, with significant contributions from industries such as tourism, agriculture, and manufacturing. The city has also seen growth in sectors like renewable energy and technology. Local businesses and international investments have helped modernize the economy, providing job opportunities and fostering economic development.

Fact 58: Tourism Economy

Tourism is a cornerstone of Marrakech's economy, attracting millions of visitors annually. The city's rich history, stunning architecture, vibrant markets, and cultural festivals draw tourists from around the world. This influx of visitors supports local businesses, hotels, restaurants, and tour operators, making tourism a vital economic driver for the city.

Fact 59: Artisan Crafts

Artisan crafts are an essential part of Marrakech's economy, reflecting the city's rich cultural heritage. Skilled craftsmen produce handmade goods such as carpets, pottery, leatherwork, and jewelry. These crafts are sold in local markets and exported internationally, contributing to the preservation of traditional skills and providing livelihoods for many artisans.

Fact 60: Local Markets

Local markets, or souks, are bustling centers of commerce in Marrakech. These markets offer a wide variety of products, from fresh produce and spices to clothing and household goods. Souks like Souk Semmarine and the Spice Market are not only vital for the local economy but also serve as major attractions for tourists seeking an authentic Moroccan shopping experience.

Chapter 13: Festivals and Events

- Fact 61: Marrakech International Film Festival

- Fact 62: Fishing Industry

- Fact 63: Shipbuilding and Maritime Industry

- Fact 64: Technological Innovations

- Fact 65: Tourism Industry

Fact 61: Marrakech International Film Festival

The Marrakech International Film Festival, inaugurated in 2001, stands as a premier event in Africa's cinematic landscape. Drawing acclaimed filmmakers, actors, and cinephiles globally, it serves as a vibrant platform for cultural dialogue and discovery. With its eclectic film lineup, the festival not only celebrates established names but also nurtures emerging talent, fostering creativity and innovation in the film industry.

Fact 62: National Festival of Popular Arts

The National Festival of Popular Arts, an annual extravaganza in Marrakech, embodies Morocco's cultural tapestry with fervent celebrations. This lively festival showcases traditional music, dance, and theatrical displays from across Morocco, highlighting the nation's artistic diversity. It serves as a crucial platform for local artists to exhibit their skills, ensuring the preservation and appreciation of Morocco's rich cultural heritage.

Fact 63: Youssef Aadam Music Festival

The Youssef Aadam Music Festival is a popular event in Marrakech that celebrates contemporary and traditional Moroccan music. Named after the renowned musician, the festival features performances by local and international artists, workshops, and cultural activities. It fosters a sense of community and promotes the appreciation of Morocco's musical heritage.

Fact 64: Cultural and Heritage Festivals

Marrakech hosts numerous cultural and heritage festivals throughout the year, highlighting the city's diverse history and traditions. These events include the Marrakech Biennale, focusing on contemporary art and culture, and the Marrakech Folklore Festival, celebrating traditional music, dance, and crafts. These festivals provide an immersive cultural experience for locals and visitors alike.

Fact 65: Seasonal Markets and Fairs

Seasonal markets and fairs are integral to Marrakech's cultural calendar. Events like the Marrakech Date Festival and the Olive Festival celebrate local agricultural products and traditional farming practices. These markets offer a variety of goods, from fresh produce to handmade crafts, and provide a lively atmosphere for socializing and cultural exchange.

- **Chapter 14: Food and Cuisine**

- Fact 66: ducational Institutions

- Fact 67: Historical Schools

- Fact 68: Research and Academia

- Fact 69: Cultural Education

- Fact 70: Language and Dialects

Fact 66: Educational Institutions

Marrakech is home to several prestigious educational institutions, including universities, vocational schools, and international schools. Cadi Ayyad University is the largest public university in the city, known for its strong programs in science, technology, and humanities, contributing significantly to the region's academic landscape.

Fact 67. Historical Schools

Marrakech has a rich history of education, with many historical schools (madrasas) that date back centuries. The Ben Youssef Madrasa, founded in the 14th century, is one of the most famous. It served as an Islamic college and is renowned for its exquisite architecture and detailed carvings. The madrasa was a center of learning and scholarship, attracting students from across the Islamic world.

Fact 68: Research and Academia

Research and academia in Marrakech are thriving, with institutions like the University of Marrakech focusing on various fields including environmental science, renewable energy, and cultural studies. These research initiatives help address local and global challenges, fostering innovation and development in the region. Collaborative projects and partnerships with international universities promote knowledge exchange and advanced research opportunities.

Fact 69: Cultural Education

Cultural education is an integral part of the learning experience in Marrakech. Schools and cultural centers emphasize the importance of preserving and understanding Moroccan heritage, including traditional arts, crafts, music, and dance, ensuring that young generations appreciate and continue the rich cultural legacy. Programs often include hands-on workshops and community events, providing students with immersive experiences. This approach helps foster a deep sense of pride and connection to their cultural roots.

Fact 70: Language and Dialects

Marrakech is a multilingual city where Arabic and Berber (Tamazight) are the primary languages spoken. French is also widely used, particularly in education and business. Language education in schools often includes these languages, promoting multilingual proficiency and cultural exchange among students. The diverse linguistic environment of Marrakech enriches communication and understanding, reflecting the city's vibrant cultural tapestry. add one line

Chapter 15: Transportation in Marrakech

- Fact 71: Public Transport

- Fact 72: Traditional Modes of Transport

- Fact 73: Modern Infrastructure

- Fact 74: Bicycle and Walking Routes

- Fact 75: Future Transportation Plans

Fact 71: Public Transport

Marrakech offers a variety of public transport options, including buses and taxis. The city's bus network is extensive, providing affordable and convenient travel within the city and to nearby regions. Taxis, both petit and grand, are widely available, offering flexible transportation options for locals and tourists. Additionally, ride-hailing services have become increasingly popular, adding to the convenience of getting around the city.

Fact 72: Traditional Modes of Transport

Traditional modes of transport, such as horse-drawn carriages (calèches), are a charming and popular way to explore Marrakech. These carriages provide a leisurely tour of the city's main attractions, allowing passengers to experience Marrakech's unique blend of old and new. It's a nostalgic journey that offers a glimpse into the city's rich history while traversing its bustling streets and historic landmarks.

Fact 73: Modern Infrastructure

Marrakech has invested in modern infrastructure to support its growing population and tourism industry. The city has well-maintained roads, an international airport, and plans for a tramway system to further enhance urban mobility. These developments aim to improve connectivity and accessibility for residents and visitors alike, ensuring sustainable growth and efficient transportation networks across the city.

Fact 74: Bicycle and Walking Routes

Bicycling and walking are encouraged in Marrakech, with dedicated paths and pedestrian-friendly areas. The city's relatively flat terrain makes it ideal for cycling, and many areas, such as the Medina, are best explored on foot. Efforts to promote sustainable transport options are ongoing, reflecting Marrakech's commitment to reducing carbon footprints and enhancing the urban environment for both residents and visitors.

Fact 75: Future Transportation Plans

Future transportation plans for Marrakech include expanding the public transit system and introducing more eco-friendly transport options. Projects such as the proposed tramway and electric buses aim to reduce traffic congestion and minimize environmental impact, aligning with the city's vision for sustainable urban development. These initiatives are expected to enhance mobility and accessibility across Marrakech, catering to the needs of its growing population and increasing number of visitors.

Chapter 16: Arts and Crafts

- Fact 76: Pottery and Ceramics

- Fact 77: Textile and Carpet Weaving

- .Fact 78: Metalwork and Jewelry

- Fact 79: Woodwork and Furniture

- Fact 80: Contemporary Art

Fact 76: Pottery and Ceramics

Marrakech's pottery and ceramics are not only admired for their intricate designs and vibrant colors but also for the skilled craftsmanship that goes into each piece. Artisans meticulously hand-craft and glaze these ceramics, drawing inspiration from centuries-old Islamic art motifs and geometric patterns, ensuring each piece tells a story of Marrakech's cultural richness and artistic heritage.

Fact 77: Textile and Carpet Weaving

Textile and carpet weaving in Marrakech represent a deep-seated tradition, where artisans skillfully create Berber rugs and silk fabrics using techniques passed down through generations. These textiles not only showcase Marrakech's rich cultural heritage but also serve as intricate pieces of art, reflecting the city's vibrant colors and patterns inspired by Moroccan landscapes and traditions.

Fact 78: Metalwork and Jewelry

Metalwork and jewelry craftsmanship in Marrakech reflect a fusion of Berber, Arab, and Andalusian influences, creating pieces that are not just ornamental but also imbued with cultural symbolism and historical significance. These artisans skillfully blend traditional techniques with contemporary designs, ensuring each piece tells a story of Marrakech's rich heritage and artistic expression.

Fact 79: Woodwork and Furniture

Marrakech's woodwork and furniture industry is celebrated for its craftsmanship in using local woods such as cedar and walnut. These materials are meticulously crafted into intricate carvings and inlays, adorning everything from architectural elements like doors and ceilings to the ornate furnishings found in riads and palaces, showcasing the city's enduring artistic traditions and skill.

Fact 80: Contemporary Art

Marrakech's vibrant contemporary art scene is evident in its galleries and exhibitions, which feature a dynamic range of works by both local and international artists. From avant-garde sculptures to thought-provoking multimedia installations, these artistic expressions not only celebrate cultural diversity but also engage with global themes, enriching the city's cultural landscape and fostering creative dialogue.

- **Chapter 17: Sustainable Development**

- Fact 81: Engineering Marvels

- Fact 82: Renewable Energy Projects

- Fact 83: Digital Innovations

- Fact 84: Start-up Ecosystem

- Fact 85: Technological Hubs

Fact 81: Engineering Marvels

Engineering Marvels: Marrakech boasts engineering marvels such as the Menara Gardens irrigation system, which dates back centuries and demonstrates advanced water management techniques. Another notable example is the intricate qanat systems, ancient underground aqueducts that have efficiently provided water to the city and surrounding areas for centuries, showcasing early hydraulic engineering prowess.

Fact 82: Renewable Energy Projects

Renewable Energy Projects: Marrakech is advancing in renewable energy with projects like the Noor Ouarzazate Solar Complex, one of the world's largest solar power plants, contributing significantly to Morocco's renewable energy goals. Additionally, the city is exploring wind energy projects in the region, harnessing the strong coastal winds to further diversify its renewable energy portfolio.

Fact 83: Digital Innovations

Digital Innovations: The city is fostering digital innovations in areas like e-commerce, mobile technology, and digital payments, enhancing connectivity and convenience for residents and businesses alike. Initiatives include smart city technologies that improve urban management and infrastructure, positioning Marrakech as a leader in digital transformation in Morocco.

Fact 84: Start-up Ecosystem

Start-up Ecosystem: Marrakech is nurturing a vibrant start-up ecosystem with initiatives like the Marrakech Biennale for startups, fostering entrepreneurship and innovation in various sectors. Co-working spaces and incubators provide support to emerging businesses, attracting local and international talent to contribute to Marrakech's economic growth and technological advancement.

Fact 85: Technological Hubs

Technological Hubs: Marrakech is home to technological hubs like CFC (Casablanca Finance City), attracting tech companies and fostering collaboration in research, development, and innovation. These hubs serve as catalysts for economic diversification and job creation, contributing to Morocco's broader technological landscape and global competitiveness.

Chapter 18: Sustainable Development in Marrakech

- Fact 86: MEco-Friendly Practices

- Fact 87: Conservation Projects

- Fact 88: Renewable Energy Initiatives

- Fact 89: Renewable Energy Initiatives

- Fact 90: Green Building Practices

Fact 86: Eco-Friendly Practices

Marrakech's eco-friendly practices extend to sustainable tourism initiatives that emphasize responsible travel behaviors and the preservation of natural landscapes. Additionally, local businesses are encouraged to adopt environmentally friendly practices to further support the city's commitment to sustainability.

Fact 87: Conservation Projects

The city engages in conservation projects to protect its natural heritage, including initiatives focused on preserving biodiversity, restoring ecosystems, and creating green spaces within urban areas. Programs such as the reforestation of the Atlas Mountains and the protection of endangered species like the Barbary macaque highlight Marrakech's dedication to environmental preservation.

Fact 88: The Nobel Peace Prize

Marrakech is committed to renewable energy initiatives, exemplified by projects like the Noor Ouarzazate Solar Complex, which aims to harness solar power to meet energy demands sustainably. The city also invests in wind energy and other renewable sources to diversify its energy portfolio. These initiatives not only reduce reliance on fossil fuels but also contribute to Morocco's overall goal of increasing its renewable energy capacity.

Fact 89: Waste Management

Efforts in waste management include recycling programs, waste segregation at source, and public education campaigns to reduce landfill waste and promote responsible disposal practices. The city also collaborates with local businesses and organizations to implement waste reduction strategies and improve the overall efficiency of waste management systems.

Fact 90: Green Building Practices

Marrakech is increasingly adopting green building practices, incorporating energy-efficient designs, sustainable materials, and eco-friendly construction methods. The city's architectural developments aim to reduce environmental impact while promoting sustainable urban growth. New buildings often feature solar panels, green roofs, and efficient water usage systems to support environmental sustainability.

Chapter 19: Educational Reforms in Marrakech

- Fact 91: Norwegian Folklore

- Fact 92: Famous Norwegian Inventions

- Fact 93: Unique Architectural Styles

- Fact 94: Norwegian Work Culture

- Fact 95: Prominent NGOs in Norway

Fact 91: Educational System Reforms

Marrakech has undertaken significant educational system reforms aimed at improving the quality and accessibility of education. These reforms include updating curricula, enhancing teacher training programs, and increasing investment in educational infrastructure. The goal is to provide a more holistic and inclusive education that meets the needs of a diverse student population.

Fact 92: STEM Education Initiatives

To prepare students for the future, Marrakech has introduced STEM (Science, Technology, Engineering, and Mathematics) education initiatives. These programs emphasize hands-on learning, critical thinking, and problem-solving skills. By encouraging interest in STEM fields from an early age, the city aims to foster innovation and competitiveness in the global economy.

Fact 93: Cultural Education Programs

Cultural education programs in Marrakech focus on preserving and promoting the city's rich heritage. Schools incorporate traditional arts, crafts, music, and dance into their curricula, ensuring that students appreciate and continue the cultural legacy. These programs help to foster a sense of identity and pride among young Moroccans.

Fact 94: Language Learning Initiatives

Marrakech has implemented language learning initiatives to promote multilingualism. Arabic and Berber (Tamazight) are taught alongside French and English, enhancing students' language skills and cultural understanding. These initiatives aim to equip students with the linguistic abilities needed for both local and international communication. The diverse linguistic education helps students appreciate the city's cultural heritage and prepares them for global opportunities.

Fact 95: Educational Technology

The integration of educational technology in Marrakech's schools is transforming the learning experience. Digital tools, e-learning platforms, and interactive resources are used to enhance teaching methods and engage students. These advancements aim to create a more dynamic and accessible educational environment, preparing students for the digital age.

Chapter 20: Future Prospects

- Fact 96: Technological Advancements

- Fact 97: Sustainable Development

- Fact 98: Educational Reforms

- Fact 99: Economic Growth

- Fact 100: Taiwan's Role in the Global Community

Fact 96: Technological Advancements

Marrakech is poised for significant technological advancements, with ongoing investments in smart city initiatives and digital infrastructure. The focus is on developing high-tech industries, enhancing internet connectivity, and fostering innovation through tech hubs and startup incubators. These advancements aim to position Marrakech as a leading technology center in the region.

Fact 97: Sustainable Development

The future of Marrakech includes a strong commitment to sustainable development. Plans involve expanding renewable energy projects, increasing green spaces, and implementing eco-friendly urban planning. Initiatives such as promoting sustainable tourism and environmentally conscious practices among businesses are central to Marrakech's vision of a sustainable and resilient city.

Fact 98: Educational Reforms

Educational reforms in Marrakech continue to evolve, with a focus on improving access to quality education and adapting curricula to meet future challenges. Emphasis is placed on STEM education, multilingual proficiency, and integrating technology into classrooms. These reforms aim to equip students with the skills needed for the modern workforce and global economy.

Fact 99: Economic Growth

Marrakech's economic growth prospects are promising, driven by sectors such as tourism, renewable energy, and technology. Efforts to diversify the economy include supporting small and medium-sized enterprises (SMEs) and attracting foreign investment. The city's strategic location and cultural appeal make it an attractive destination for business and investment, fostering sustained economic development.

Fact 100: Taiwan's Role in the Global Community

Taiwan's role in the global community, including its contributions to technological innovation and sustainable practices, serves as an inspiration for Marrakech. Collaborative projects and knowledge exchange between Marrakech and Taiwan can enhance Marrakech's development initiatives. Taiwan's experience in areas like smart cities and renewable energy offers valuable insights for Marrakech's future growth.

Conclusion

✹ As we conclude "100 Amazing Facts About Marrakech for Young Readers," we hope you've been captivated by the magic, history, and vibrant culture of this enchanting city. From bustling souks to majestic palaces, Marrakech is a treasure trove of wonders. Let its rich traditions and welcoming people inspire your own adventures. Thank you for joining us on this colorful journey, and may the spirit of Marrakech spark your imagination and curiosity for many more adventures to come! ✹